THE E

of

SELF TEST JOURNAL

THE EVALUATION

of

SELF TEST JOURNAL

A Resource To Be Used With The Book,

The Evaluation of Self Test

Created by

ANTHONY EUGENE VANN

Table of Contents

Introduction

This Journal is to be used in conjunction with the book, The Evaluation of Self Test by Anthony Eugene Vann. It is my sincere hope and prayer that this journal and the accompanying book can be used to create whatever you want within your Self or your life.

This journal is another, proven example of the creative nature of The Evaluation of Self Test. The thoughts, ideas and concepts that are presented in the book are the same thoughts, ideas and concepts that were used to create this journal.

You can create whatever you want for your Self as well if you can apply what is provided in the book to your unique situation. But to do so you must make a choice; a choice to be patient, determined and steadfast in your efforts until the changes you desire, manifests into reality.

This journal was created as a resource to write all of your answers to the questions and quizzes presented in the book. In addition, you should write what you experience mentally, physically, emotionally, and spiritually during the exercises in the journaling section. Quotes from the book have also been added. They are provided to serve as reminders of the thoughts, ideas and concepts provided in the book.

This journal, if used as intended, will ensure you pass the test and it will contain a wealth of information to change anything about your Self or life when you complete The Evaluation of Self Test.

The Journal includes sections to write your

- ➢ Purpose Statement
- ➢ Categories of Life Situations
- ➢ Philosophy Statement and Principles
- ➢ Measured Action Plan (MAP)
- ➢ Self-Induced Mental Obstacles
- ➢ Matters of Major Importance
- ➢ Problematic Life Situations and more

> Top Ten and Most Impactful Areas of Your BEACH
> Journaling / Periods of Reflection / Meditation Notes

Self-Evaluation is a lifetime journey. Review this journal annually to reflect on what you learned about your Self. Additional space has also been provided for you to write your findings during annual reviews or to repeat the test. Use the space provided in whatever manner you choose. Anything you write will add to your wealth of information to use now or at some other moment in time.

Answer the questions to the test truthfully. Pause and or meditate on each question before you answer it. This will provide you with a clear picture of your Self.

What is written in this journal may paint an unattractive portrait of your Self and the life you are living. But it is my hope that you, as the artist, can change that portrait with a little touchup or an entire makeover. You are in control of the portrait. But there will not be a portrait if you don't fill this journal with honest answers as you complete The Evaluation of Self Test.

Pause.....

Smile.........Pause

Slowly, Take 3 Deep Breaths......Pause

Relax, Smile, Slowly Breathe Deeply.........Pause

Let's Begin!

Expectations

Set your expectations prior to starting, The Evaluation of Self Test. At the end of the book, review them to reflect on reasons why they were or were not experienced.

_____

_____

_____

_____

_____

_____

_____

_____

_____

_____

_____

_____

_____

_____

_____

_____

_____

_____

_____

_____

_____

_____

_____

_____

Chapter One ~ The Need For Self-Evaluation

~~~~~~~~~~~~~~

Answers to the Test / Journaling

~~~~~~~~~~~~~~~~~~~~~~~~~~~~

"Real Change Has To Begin, Within Your Self" A.E.V.

_____

_____

_____

_____

_____

_____

_____

_____

_____

_____

_____

_____

_____

_____

_____

_____

_____

_____

_____

_____

_____

_____

_____

_____

Chapter One ~ The Need For Self-Evaluation

Answers to the Test / Journaling

"Tests Give Us a Point of Reference" A.E.V.

_____

_____

_____

_____

_____

_____

_____

_____

_____

_____

_____

_____

_____

_____

_____

_____

_____

_____

_____

_____

_____

_____

_____

Chapter One ~ The Need For Self-Evaluation

~~~~~~~~~~~~~~~~

Answers to the Test / Journaling

~~~~~~~~~~~~~~~~~~~~~~~~~~~~~~~~

"Your Goal Should Be to Bring Order Into Each Area of Your Life
If and Where It Does Not Already Exist" A.E.V.

_____

_____

_____

_____

_____

_____

_____

_____

_____

_____

_____

_____

_____

_____

_____

_____

_____

_____

_____

_____

_____

_____

Chapter One ~ The Need For Self-Evaluation

Answers to the Test / Journaling

"Work Harder On Your Self, Than You Do On Your Job" Jim Rohn

Chapter One ~ The Need For Self-Evaluation

~~~~~~~~~~~~~~~~

Answers to the Test / Journaling

~~~~~~~~~~~~~~~~~~~~~~~~~~~~

"Take Responsibility and Ownership For Your Life" A.E.V.

_____

_____

_____

_____

_____

_____

_____

_____

_____

_____

_____

_____

_____

_____

_____

_____

_____

_____

_____

_____

_____

_____

Chapter One ~ The Need For Self-Evaluation

Answers to the Test / Journaling

*"Whenever You Fail At Something, You Must
Find An Interesting Lesson (FAIL) In That Failure"* A.E.V.

Chapter Two ~ Knowing Your Purpose

~~~~~~~~~~~~~~~~~~

Answers to the Test / Journaling

~~~~~~~~~~~~~~~~~~~~~~~~~~~~~~~~

"Life Is About Repetition – Repetition of Thoughts,
Emotions and Activities" A.E.V.

_____

_____

_____

_____

_____

_____

_____

_____

_____

_____

_____

_____

_____

_____

_____

_____

_____

_____

_____

_____

_____

_____

_____

Chapter Two ~ Knowing Your Purpose

~~~~~~~~~~~~~

Answers to the Test / Journaling

~~~~~~~~~~~~~~~~~~~~~~~~~~~~~~~~~~~

"Your Philosophy Will Establish The Principles By Which You Act and Behave While You Exist and Live With Purpose" A.E.V.

_____

_____

_____

_____

_____

_____

_____

_____

_____

_____

_____

_____

_____

_____

_____

_____

_____

_____

_____

_____

_____

Chapter Two ~ Knowing Your Purpose

~~~~~~~~~~~~~~~~

Answers to the Test / Journaling

~~~~~~~~~~~~~~~~~~~~~~~~~~~~~~~~~~~~

"We As Human Beings Are Creative Through Our Thoughts, Emotions, Voice and Body" A.E.V.

_____

_____

_____

_____

_____

_____

_____

_____

_____

_____

_____

_____

_____

_____

_____

_____

_____

_____

_____

_____

_____

_____

Chapter Two ~ Knowing Your Purpose

Answers to the Test / Journaling

*"The Purpose of This Creative Force Within Us Is To Create
While Existing As Physical Beings Until Our Physical Life Ends"* A.E.V.

Chapter Two ~ Knowing Your Purpose

~~~~~~~~~~~~~~~

Answers to the Test / Journaling

~~~~~~~~~~~~~~~~~~~~~~~~~~~~~~~

"You Must Learn How To Control Your Mind
By Bringing Your Thought Process to a Temporary End
Any Time You Wish" A.E.V.

_____

_____

_____

_____

_____

_____

_____

_____

_____

_____

_____

_____

_____

_____

_____

_____

_____

_____

_____

Chapter Two ~ Knowing Your Purpose

~~~~~~~~~~~~~~~~

Answers to the Test / Journaling

~~~~~~~~~~~~~~~~~~~~~~~~~~~~~~~~~

"Existence and Being Are Internal and Eternal" A.E.V.

Chapter Two ~ Knowing Your Purpose

~~~~~~~~~~~~~~~~

Answers to the Test / Journaling

~~~~~~~~~~~~~~~~~~~~~~~~~~~~~~~~~~~

"Knowing You Purpose Focuses Your Life.
It Concentrates Your Effort and Energy On What's Important" Rick Warren

_____

_____

_____

_____

_____

_____

_____

_____

_____

_____

_____

_____

_____

_____

_____

_____

_____

_____

_____

_____

Chapter Two ~ Knowing Your Purpose

~~~~~~~~~~~~~~~~~

Answers to the Test / Journaling

~~~~~~~~~~~~~~~~~~~~~~~~~~~~~~~~

*"Focus On One Purpose For Your Self To Concentrate On
While Resisting The Urges And Distractions That Life Presents You
As The Situations In Your Life Align With Your Purpose" A.E.V.*

_____

_____

_____

_____

_____

_____

_____

_____

_____

_____

_____

_____

_____

_____

_____

_____

_____

_____

_____

_____

Chapter Two ~ Knowing Your Purpose

~~~~~~~~~~~~~~~~~~

Answers to the Test / Journaling

~~~~~~~~~~~~~~~~~~~~~~~~~~~~~~~

"Exist as a Being of Happiness and Peace" A.E.V.

Chapter Two ~ Knowing Your Purpose

~~~~~~~~~~~~~~~~

Answers to the Test / Journaling

~~~~~~~~~~~~~~~~~~~~~~~~~~~~~~~~

"Emotions are Creative" A.E.V.

Chapter Two ~ Knowing Your Purpose

~~~~~~~~~~~~~~~~~~~

Answers to Quiz 1

~~~~~~~~~~~~~~~~~~~~~~~~~~~~~~~

Chapter Two ~ Knowing Your Purpose

~~~~~~~~~~~~~~~~~

Answers to Quiz 1

~~~~~~~~~~~~~~~~~~~~~~~~~~~~~~~~~

Chapter Two ~ Knowing Your Purpose

~~~~~~~~~~~~~~~~~~~~~

Answers to Quiz 1

~~~~~~

Chapter Two ~ Knowing Your Purpose

~~~~~~~~~~~~~~~~~

Answers to Quiz 1

~~~~~~~~~~~~~~~~~~~~~~~~~~~~~~~

Chapter Two ~ Knowing Your Purpose

Answers to Quiz 1

Chapter Two ~ Knowing Your Purpose

~~~~~~~~~~~~~~~~~

Answers to Quiz 1

~~~~~~~~~~~~~~~~~~~~~~~~~~~~~~~~

Chapter Two ~ Knowing Your Purpose

Answers to Quiz 1

_____

_____

_____

_____

_____

_____

_____

_____

_____

_____

_____

_____

_____

_____

_____

_____

_____

_____

_____

_____

_____

_____

_____

Chapter Two ~ Knowing Your Purpose

~~~~~~~~~~~~~~~~~~

Answers to Quiz 1

~~~~~~~~~~~~~~~~~~~~~~~~~~~~~~~~~

Chapter Three ~ Understanding Your Life Situation Part One

~~~~~~~~~~~~~~~~~

Answers to the Test / Journaling

~~~~~~~~~~~~~~~~~~~~~~~~~~~~~~~

"Your Life Situation Is All The Situations You Find Your Self In Today,
In Every Area of Your Life" A.E.V.

_____

_____

_____

_____

_____

_____

_____

_____

_____

_____

_____

_____

_____

_____

_____

_____

_____

_____

_____

_____

_____

Chapter Three ~ Understanding Your Life Situation Part One

~~~~~~~~~~~~~~~~~~~~~

Answers to the Test / Journaling

~~~~~~~~~~~~~~~~~~~~~~~~~~~~~~~~~~~~~

"The Person That Exists Within Their Purpose Has Learned How To Manage The Various Situations In Their Life Better; With Less Stress, Fear, Anger, or Worry" A.E.V.

Chapter Three ~ Understanding Your Life Situation Part One

~~~~~~~~~~~~~~~~~

Answers to the Test / Journaling

~~~~~~~~~~~~~~~~~~~~~~~~~~~~~~~~~

"Problematic Life Situations Move The Focus of Your Attention and Your Emotional State Away From Your Purpose" A.E.V.

_____

_____

_____

_____

_____

_____

_____

_____

_____

_____

_____

_____

_____

_____

_____

_____

_____

_____

_____

_____

_____

_____

_____

Chapter Three ~ Understanding Your Life Situation Part One

~~~~~~~~~~~~~~~~

Answers to the Test / Journaling

~~~~~~~~~~~~~~~~~~~~~~~~~~~~~~~~~~~

"Situation Management Is The Process of Managing Each of Your Life Situations With The Time and Attention That Is Necessary To Align Them With Your Purpose" A.E.V.

Chapter Three ~ Understanding Your Life Situation Part One

~~~~~~~~~~~~~~~~

Answers to the Test / Journaling

~~~~~~~~~~~~~~~~~~~~~~~~~~~~~~

"The Four Phases of Situation Management are Opportunities For Change, Making Conscious Choices, Making The Final Decision and Monitoring and Evaluating The New Situation" A.E.V.

_____

_____

_____

_____

_____

_____

_____

_____

_____

_____

_____

_____

_____

_____

_____

_____

_____

_____

_____

_____

Chapter Three ~ Understanding Your Life Situation Part One

Answers to the Test / Journaling

"By Using What I Refer to as The 5W1H Method of Brainstorming, You Can Solve Almost Any Problem In Your Life" A.E.V.

Chapter Three ~ Understanding Your Life Situation Part One

Answers to the Test / Journaling

"By Making Better Choices, You Improve Your Self and Your Life, Reduce or Eliminate Problematic Situations, and Align All of Your Life Situations With Your Purpose" A.E.V.

_____

_____

_____

_____

_____

_____

_____

_____

_____

_____

_____

_____

_____

_____

_____

_____

_____

_____

_____

_____

_____

Chapter Three ~ Understanding Your Life Situation Part One

~~~~~~~~~~~~~~

Answers to the Test / Journaling

~~~~~~~~~~~~~~~~~~~~~~~~~~~~~~

"The Five Areas of Conditioning Are Beliefs, Environment, Actions, Conditioned Responses and Habits (BEACH)" A.E.V.

Chapter Three ~ Understanding Your Life Situation Part One

~~~~~~~~~~~~~~~~~

Answers to the Test / Journaling

~~~~~~~~~~~~~~~~~~~~~~~~~~~~~~~

"You Can Change The Conditioning of Your Self If You Change Any Area of Your BEACH" A.E.V.

_____

_____

_____

_____

_____

_____

_____

_____

_____

_____

_____

_____

_____

_____

_____

_____

_____

_____

_____

_____

_____

_____

Chapter Three ~ Understanding Your Life Situation Part One

~~~~~~~~~~~~~~~~

Answers to the Test / Journaling

~~~~~~~~~~~~~~~~~~~~~~~~~~~~

"A Belief Is A Thought You Keep Thinking" Abraham Hicks

_____

_____

_____

_____

_____

_____

_____

_____

_____

_____

_____

_____

_____

_____

_____

_____

_____

_____

_____

_____

_____

_____

Chapter Four ~ Understanding Your Life Situation Part Two

~~~~~~~~~~~~~~~

Answers to the Test / Journaling

~~~~~~~~~~~~~~~~~~~~~~~~~~~~~~~~~~

"This Is The Time For Change, A Time For Action, For Transformation" A.E.V.

_____

_____

_____

_____

_____

_____

_____

_____

_____

_____

_____

_____

_____

_____

_____

_____

_____

_____

_____

_____

Chapter Four ~ Understanding Your Life Situation Part Two

~~~~~~~~~~~~~~

Answers to the Test / Journaling

~~~~~~~~~~~~~~~~~~~~~~~~~~~~~~~~

"Take Responsibility For Your Life By Using Your Power Of Choice" A.E.V.

Chapter Four ~ Understanding Your Life Situation Part Two

~~~~~~~~~~~~~~~

Answers to the Test / Journaling

~~~~~~~~~~~~~~~~~~~~~~~~~~~~

"Life Is In A Constant State of Change That Affects
All People, Places, and Things" A.E.V.

_____

_____

_____

_____

_____

_____

_____

_____

_____

_____

_____

_____

_____

_____

_____

_____

_____

_____

_____

_____

_____

_____

_____

_____

Chapter Four ~ Understanding Your Life Situation Part Two

~~~~~~~~~~~~~~~~

Answers to the Test / Journaling

~~~~~~~~~~~~~~~~~~~~~~~~~~~~~~~~~~~

*"Make The Best Decision You Can Based On The Information You Have
and Move Forward Until The Situation Has Changed
and Is More In Alignment With Your Purpose" A.E.V.*

Chapter Four ~ Understanding Your Life Situation Part Two

~~~~~~~~~~~~~~~~~

Answers to the Test / Journaling

~~~~~~~~~~~~~~~~~~~~~~~~~~~~~~~~~~

"Don't Build A Foundation For Situation Management
That Can't Stand The Test of Time" A.E.V.

_____

_____

_____

_____

_____

_____

_____

_____

_____

_____

_____

_____

_____

_____

_____

_____

_____

_____

_____

_____

_____

_____

Chapter Four ~ Understanding Your Life Situation Part Two

~~~~~~~~~~~~~~~~

Answers to the Test / Journaling

~~~~~~~~~~~~~~~~~~~~~~~~~~~~~~~~~~~~~

"You Must Continually Monitor How The People, Places, And Things Involved In Your Decision Are Affected By It" A.E.V.

_____

_____

_____

_____

_____

_____

_____

_____

_____

_____

_____

_____

_____

_____

_____

_____

_____

_____

_____

_____

_____

_____

_____

_____

_____

Chapter Four ~ Understanding Your Life Situation Part Two

~~~~~~~~~~~~~~~~~~~

Answers to the Test / Journaling

~~~~~~~~~~~~~~~~~~~~~~~~~~~~~~~~~~~

"Failure Is The Greatest Teaching Tool Available To Us" A.E.V.

Chapter Four ~ Understanding Your Life Situation Part Two

~~~~~~~~~~

Answers to the Test / Journaling

~~~~~~~~~~~~~~~~~~~~~~~~~~~

"Your Philosophy Will Establish The Principles By Which You Act and Behave While You Exist and Live With Purpose" A.E.V.

_____

_____

_____

_____

_____

_____

_____

_____

_____

_____

_____

_____

_____

_____

_____

_____

_____

_____

_____

_____

_____

_____

Chapter Four ~ Understanding Your Life Situation Part Two

~~~~~~~~~~~~~~~~

Answers to the Test / Journaling

~~~~~~~~~~~~~~~~~~~~~~~~~~~~~~~

"You Principles Will Establish The Plan of Action By Which You Change Any Situation In Your Life That Is Not In Alignment With Your Purpose" A.E.V.

_____

_____

_____

_____

_____

_____

_____

_____

_____

_____

_____

_____

_____

_____

_____

_____

_____

_____

_____

_____

_____

_____

Chapter Four ~ Understanding Your Life Situation Part Two

~~~~~~~~~~~~~~~

Answers to the Test / Journaling

~~~~~~~~~~~~~~~~~~~~~~~~~~~~~~~~

"You Want A Philosophy That Creates A Mindset, An Attitude or Demeanor – A Way to Live and Act; Not A Goal" A.E.V.

_____

_____

_____

_____

_____

_____

_____

_____

_____

_____

_____

_____

_____

_____

_____

_____

_____

_____

_____

_____

_____

_____

_____

Chapter Four ~ Understanding Your Life Situation Part Two

~~~~~~~~~~~~~~~

Answers to Quiz 2

~~~~~~~~~~~~~~~~~~~~~~~~~~~~~~~~

Chapter Four ~ Understanding Your Life Situation Part Two

~~~~~~~~~~~~~~~~~

Answers to Quiz 2

~~~~~~~~~~~~~~~~~~~~~~~~~~~~~~~~~~~~~

Chapter Four ~ Understanding Your Life Situation Part Two

~~~~~~~~~~~~~~~~

Answers to Quiz 2

~~~~~~~~~~~~~~~~~~~~~~~~~~~~~~~~~~~~~~

Chapter Four ~ Understanding Your Life Situation Part Two

~~~~~~~~~~~~~~~~

Answers to Quiz 2

~~~~~~~~~~~~~~~~~~~~~~~~~~~~

Chapter Four ~ Understanding Your Life Situation Part Two

~~~~~~~~~~~~~~~~

Answers to Quiz 2

~~~~~~~~~~~~~~~~~~~~~~~~~~~~

Chapter Four ~ Understanding Your Life Situation Part Two

Answers to Quiz 2

Chapter Four ~ Understanding Your Life Situation Part Two

~~~~~~~~~~~~~~~~~

Answers to Quiz 2

~~~~~~~~~~~~~~~~~~~~~~~~~~~~~~

Chapter Four ~ Understanding Your Life Situation Part Two

~~~~~~~~~~~~~~~~~

Answers to Quiz 2

~~~~~~~~~~~~~~~~~~~~~~~~~~~~~~

Chapter Five ~ Understanding
The Importance of Goals

~~~~~~~~~~~~~~~~~

Answers to the Test / Journaling

~~~~~~~~~~~~~~~~~~~~~~~~~~~~~

"When You Set A Goal, You Are Setting A Plan of Action In Motion" A.E.V.

Chapter Five ~ Understanding
The Importance of Goals

~~~~~~~~~~~~~~~~~

Answers to the Test / Journaling

~~~~~~~~~~~~~~~~~~~~~~~~~~~~~~

"A Goal That Is Thought About, Visualized, Written Down and Verbally Affirmed
Has A Far Better Chance of Being Completed
Than One That Is Simply Thought About" A.E.V.

_____

_____

_____

_____

_____

_____

_____

_____

_____

_____

_____

_____

_____

_____

_____

_____

_____

_____

_____

_____

_____

_____

Chapter Five ~ Understanding
The Importance of Goals

~~~~~~~~~~~~~~~~

Answers to the Test / Journaling

~~~~~~~~~~~~~~~~~~~~~~~~~~~~~~~~

"Goals Provide A Good Opportunity To Analyze Your Life Situation" A.E.V.

Chapter Five ~ Understanding
The Importance of Goals

~~~~~~~~~~~~~~

Answers to the Test / Journaling

~~~~~~~~~~~~~~~~~~~~~~~~~~~~~~

"Goals Help You Go On After Losing Something" A.E.V.

_____

_____

_____

_____

_____

_____

_____

_____

_____

_____

_____

_____

_____

_____

_____

_____

_____

_____

_____

_____

_____

_____

_____

Chapter Five ~ Understanding
The Importance of Goals

~~~~~~~~~~~~~~~~

Answers to the Test / Journaling

~~~~~~~~~~~~~~~~~~~~~~~~~~~~~

"Goals Allow The Gifts Of All Living Spirits To Manifest Into Reality" A.E.V.

_____

_____

_____

_____

_____

_____

_____

_____

_____

_____

_____

_____

_____

_____

_____

_____

_____

_____

_____

_____

_____

_____

Chapter Five ~ Understanding
The Importance of Goals

~~~~~~~~~~~~~~~

Answers to the Test / Journaling

~~~~~~~~~~~~~~~~~~~~~~~~~~~~~~~

"Be Careful What You Become In The Pursuit of Your Goals" Jim Rohn

Chapter Five ~ Understanding
The Importance of Goals

~~~~~~~~~~~~

Answers to the Test / Journaling

~~~~~~~~~~~~~~~~~~~~~~~~

"Your MAP Will Help You Reach Your Destinations and Reach Your Goals
Faster and Easier Than If You Did Not Have It" A.E.V.

_____

_____

_____

_____

_____

_____

_____

_____

_____

_____

_____

_____

_____

_____

_____

_____

_____

_____

_____

_____

_____

Chapter Five ~ Understanding
The Importance of Goals

~~~~~~~~~~~~~~~~~

Answers to the Test / Journaling

~~~~~~~~~~~~~~~~~~~~~~~~~~~~~~~~~~

*"The Person That Exists Within Their Purpose Has Learned How To Manage
The Various Situations In Their Life Better;
With Less Stress, Fear, Anger, or Worry"* A.E.V.

_____

_____

_____

_____

_____

_____

_____

_____

_____

_____

_____

_____

_____

_____

_____

_____

_____

_____

_____

_____

_____

_____

Chapter Five ~ Understanding
The Importance of Goals

~~~~~~~~~~~~~~~~

Answers to the Test / Journaling

~~~~~~~~~~~~~~~~~~~~~~~~~~~~~~~~

"Daily, Purposeful Action Will Bring About The Greatest Amount of Change In Your Life Situations" A.E.V.

_____

_____

_____

_____

_____

_____

_____

_____

_____

_____

_____

_____

_____

_____

_____

_____

_____

_____

_____

_____

_____

_____

Chapter Five ~ Understanding
The Importance of Goals

~~~~~~~~~~~~~~

Answers to the Test / Journaling

~~~~~~~~~~~~~~~~~~~~~~~~~~~~

"The Day You Create A Goal and Set A Time/Date of Completion,
You Have Decided To Test Your Self" A.E.V.

_____

_____

_____

_____

_____

_____

_____

_____

_____

_____

_____

_____

_____

_____

_____

_____

_____

_____

_____

_____

_____

_____

Chapter Five ~ Understanding
The Importance of Goals

~~~~~~~~~~~~~~~~~~

Answers to Quiz 3

~~~~~~~~~~~~~~~~~~~~~~~~~~~~~~

_____

_____

_____

_____

_____

_____

_____

_____

_____

_____

_____

_____

_____

_____

_____

_____

_____

_____

_____

_____

_____

_____

Chapter Five ~ Understanding
The Importance of Goals

Answers to Quiz 3

Chapter Five ~ Understanding
The Importance of Goals

~~~~~~~~~~~~~~~~~~~

Answers to Quiz 3

~~~~~~~~~~~~~~~~~~~~~~~~~~~~~~

_____

_____

_____

_____

_____

_____

_____

_____

_____

_____

_____

_____

_____

_____

_____

_____

_____

_____

_____

_____

_____

_____

_____

Chapter Five ~ Understanding
The Importance of Goals

~~~~~~~~~~~~~~~~~~

Answers to Quiz 3

~~~~~~~~~~~~~~~~~~~~~~~~~~~~~~

Chapter Five ~ Understanding
The Importance of Goals

~~~~~~~~~~~~~~

Answers to Quiz 3

~~~~~~~~~~~~~~~~~~~~~~~~~~~~~

Chapter Five ~ Understanding
The Importance of Goals

~~~~~~~~~~~~~~~~~

Answers to Quiz 3

~~~~~~~~~~~~~~~~~~~~~~~~~~~~~~~

Chapter Five ~ Understanding
The Importance of Goals

~~~~~~~~~~~~~~~~~

Answers to Quiz 3

~~~~~~~~~~~~~~~~~~~~~~~~~~~~~~~~

_____

_____

_____

_____

_____

_____

_____

_____

_____

_____

_____

_____

_____

_____

_____

_____

_____

_____

_____

_____

_____

_____

_____

_____

Chapter Five ~ Understanding
The Importance of Goals

~~~~~~~~~~~~~~~~~

Answers to Quiz 3

~~~~~~~~~~~~~~~~~~~~~~~~~~~~~~~~

_____

_____

_____

_____

_____

_____

_____

_____

_____

_____

_____

_____

_____

_____

_____

_____

_____

_____

_____

_____

_____

Chapter Six ~ Living A Balanced Life

~~~~~~~~~~~~~~

Answers to the Test / Journaling

~~~~~~~~~~~~~~~~~~~~~~~~~~~~~~~~~~~

*"You Bring Balance Into Your Life When The Peace That Dwells Within You
Is Reflected On Your Face, In Your Speech,
Your Appearance, Actions, and Behavior" A.E.V.*

_____

_____

_____

_____

_____

_____

_____

_____

_____

_____

_____

_____

_____

_____

_____

_____

_____

_____

_____

Chapter Six ~ Living A Balanced Life

Answers to the Test / Journaling

"You Bring Balance Into Your Life When You Know Your Point of Reference"
A.E.V.

Chapter Six ~ Living A Balanced Life

Answers to the Test / Journaling

*"You Bring Balance Into Your Life When You Ensure You Are Being Fed
In Each Corner of Your Internal Self" A.E.V.*

Chapter Six ~ Living A Balanced Life

~~~~~~~~~~~~~~~~~

Answers to the Test / Journaling

~~~~~~~~~~~~~~~~~~~~~~~~~~~~~~~

"You Bring Balance Into Your Life When You Can Challenge and Push Through The Illusory Wall of Self-Induced Mental Obstacles" A.E.V.

Chapter Six ~ Living A Balanced Life

~~~~~~~~~~~~~~~~

Answers to the Test / Journaling

~~~~~~~~~~~~~~~~~~~~~~~~~~~~~~~~

"You Bring Balance Into Your Life When You Are Living With Purpose, When Your Choices And Decisions Are In Alignment With Your Purpose and the Focus of Your Attention Is On The Achievement of Your Goals" A.E.V.

Chapter Six ~ Living A Balanced Life

~~~~~~~~~~~~~~~~

Answers to the Test / Journaling

~~~~~~~~~~~~~~~~~~~~~~~~~~~~~~~~

"You Bring Balance Into Your Life When Each Category of Your Life Situation Is Not In A Problematic State" A.E.V.

Chapter Six ~ Living A Balanced Life

Answers to the Test / Journaling

*"You Bring Balance Into Your Life When You See The Good
In All Things and Situations" A.E.V.*

Chapter Six ~ Living A Balanced Life

~~~~~~~~~~~~~~~~~

Answers to the Test / Journaling

~~~~~~~~~~~~~~~~~~~~~~~~~~~~~~~~

"Peace of Mind Is The Result of Having A Life In Balance" A.E.V.

Chapter Six ~ Living A Balanced Life

~~~~~~~~~~~~~~~~~

Answers to the Test / Journaling

~~~~~~~~~~~~~~~~~~~~~~~~~~~~~~~~~

"A Transition Is A Period of Time Where You Change From One State of Balance To Another" A.E.V.

Chapter Six ~ Living A Balanced Life

~~~~~~~~~~~~~~~~~~

Answers to the Test / Journaling

~~~~~~~~~~~~~~~~~~~~~~~~~~~~~~~~~~

"One of the Keys To A Life of Balance Is To
Approach All Situations With Love, Peace and Understanding" A.E.V.

Chapter Six ~ Living A Balanced Life

Answers to Quiz 4

Chapter Six ~ Living A Balanced Life

Answers to Quiz 4

Chapter Six ~ Living A Balanced Life

Answers to Quiz 4

Chapter Six ~ Living A Balanced Life

Answers to Quiz 4

Chapter Six ~ Living A Balanced Life

Answers to Quiz 4

Chapter Six ~ Living A Balanced Life

Answers to Quiz 4

Chapter Six ~ Living A Balanced Life

~~~~~~~~~~~~~~~~

Answers to Quiz 4

~~~~~~~~~~~~~~~~~~~~~~~~~~~~~~~~

Chapter Six ~ Living A Balanced Life

Answers to Quiz 4

Chapter Seven ~ The Review

Test Completion ~ Purpose Statement

_____

_____

_____

_____

_____

_____

_____

_____

_____

_____

_____

_____

_____

_____

_____

_____

_____

_____

_____

_____

_____

_____

_____

_____

_____

_____

_____

_____

Chapter Seven ~ The Review

Test Completion ~ Categorized List of Life Situations

_____

_____

_____

_____

_____

_____

_____

_____

_____

_____

_____

_____

_____

_____

_____

_____

_____

_____

_____

_____

_____

_____

_____

_____

_____

_____

_____

_____

_____

_____

_____

Chapter Seven ~ The Review

Test Completion ~ Categorized List of Life Situations

_____

_____

_____

_____

_____

_____

_____

_____

_____

_____

_____

_____

_____

_____

_____

_____

_____

_____

_____

_____

_____

_____

_____

_____

_____

_____

_____

_____

_____

Chapter Seven ~ The Review

~~~~~~~~~~~~~~~

Test Completion ~ Categorized List of Life Situations

~~~~~~~~~~~~~~~~~~~~~~~~~~~~~~

_____

_____

_____

_____

_____

_____

_____

_____

_____

_____

_____

_____

_____

_____

_____

_____

_____

_____

_____

_____

_____

_____

_____

_____

Chapter Seven ~ The Review

Test Completion ~ Categorized List of Life Situations

Chapter Seven ~ The Review

Test Completion ~ Categorized List of Life Situations

Chapter Seven ~ The Review

Test Completion ~ Categorized List of Life Situations

_____

_____

_____

_____

_____

_____

_____

_____

_____

_____

_____

_____

_____

_____

_____

_____

_____

_____

_____

_____

_____

_____

_____

_____

_____

_____

_____

_____

_____

Chapter Seven ~ The Review

Test Completion ~ Your Most Problematic Life Situations

Chapter Seven ~ The Review

~~~~~~~~~~~~~~~~

Test Completion ~ Your Most Problematic
Life Situations

~~~~~~~~~~~~~~~~~~~~~~~~~~~~~~~~

Chapter Seven ~ The Review

Test Completion ~ Your Most Problematic
Life Situations

Chapter Seven ~ The Review

Test Completion ~ Your Most Problematic Life Situations

Chapter Seven ~ The Review

Test Completion ~ Your Most Problematic
Life Situations

Chapter Seven ~ The Review

Test Completion ~ Your Most Problematic
Life Situations

Chapter Seven ~ The Review

~~~~~~~~~~~~~~~~~

Test Completion ~ Top Ten List of Each Area
of Your BEACH

~~~~~~~~~~~~~~~~~~~~~~~~~~~~~~~~~

Chapter Seven ~ The Review

~~~~~~~~~~~~~~~~

Test Completion ~ Your Top Ten List
of Each Area of Your BEACH

~~~~~~~~~~~~~~~~~~~~~~~~~~~~~~~~~~

_____

_____

_____

_____

_____

_____

_____

_____

_____

_____

_____

_____

_____

_____

_____

_____

_____

_____

_____

_____

Chapter Seven ~ The Review

~~~~~~~~~~~~~~~~

Test Completion ~ Your Top Ten List
of Each Area of Your BEACH

~~~~~~~~~~~~~~~~~~~~~~~~~~~~~~~

Chapter Seven ~ The Review

Test Completion ~ Your Top Ten List
of Each Area of Your BEACH

_____

_____

_____

_____

_____

_____

_____

_____

_____

_____

_____

_____

_____

_____

_____

_____

_____

_____

_____

_____

_____

_____

Chapter Seven ~ The Review

Test Completion ~ Top Ten List of Each Area of Your BEACH

_____

_____

_____

_____

_____

_____

_____

_____

_____

_____

_____

_____

_____

_____

_____

_____

_____

_____

_____

_____

_____

_____

_____

_____

_____

Chapter Seven ~ The Review

$\sim\sim\sim\sim\sim\sim\sim\sim\sim\sim\sim$

Test Completion ~ Your Top Ten List of Each Area of Your BEACH

$\sim\sim\sim\sim\sim\sim\sim\sim\sim\sim\sim\sim\sim\sim\sim\sim\sim\sim\sim\sim\sim\sim\sim\sim$

Chapter Seven ~ The Review

~~~~~~~~~~~~~~

Test Completion ~ Your Top Ten List
of Each Area of Your BEACH

~~~~~~~~~~~~~~~~~~~~~~~~~~~~~~~~

Chapter Seven ~ The Review

~~~~~~~~~~~~~~~

Test Completion ~ Your Top Ten List
of Each Area of Your BEACH

~~~~~~~~~~~~~~~~~~~~~~~~~~~~~~~

_____

_____

_____

_____

_____

_____

_____

_____

_____

_____

_____

_____

_____

_____

_____

_____

_____

_____

_____

_____

_____

_____

Chapter Seven ~ The Review

Test Completion ~ Your Matters of Major Importance

Chapter Seven ~ The Review

Test Completion ~ Your Matters of Major Importance

Chapter Seven ~ The Review

~~~~~~~~~~~~~~

Test Completion ~ Your Matters of Major Importance

~~~~~~~~~~~~~~~~~~~~~~~~~~~~~~~~

Chapter Seven ~ The Review

Test Completion ~ Your Matters of Major Importance

Chapter Seven ~ The Review

Test Completion ~ Your Matters of Major Importance

_____

_____

_____

_____

_____

_____

_____

_____

_____

_____

_____

_____

_____

_____

_____

_____

_____

_____

_____

_____

_____

_____

_____

_____

_____

_____

_____

Chapter Seven ~ The Review

Test Completion ~ Your Philosophy and Principles

_____

_____

_____

_____

_____

_____

_____

_____

_____

_____

_____

_____

_____

_____

_____

_____

_____

_____

_____

_____

_____

_____

_____

Chapter Seven ~ The Review

~~~~~~~~~~~~~~~~~

Test Completion ~ Your Philosophy and Principles

~~~~~~~~~~~~~~~~~~~~~~~~~~~~~

Chapter Seven ~ The Review

Test Completion ~ Your Philosophy and Principles

_____

_____

_____

_____

_____

_____

_____

_____

_____

_____

_____

_____

_____

_____

_____

_____

_____

_____

_____

_____

_____

_____

_____

_____

_____

_____

_____

_____

Chapter Seven ~ The Review

Test Completion ~ Your Philosophy and Principles

Chapter Seven ~ The Review

Test Completion ~ Your Philosophy and Principles

Chapter Seven ~ The Review

Test Completion ~ Your Philosophy and Principles

Chapter Seven ~ The Review

~~~~~~~~~~~~~~~~~

Test Completion ~ Your Philosophy and Principles

~~~~~~~~~~~~~~~~~~~~~~~~~~~~~~

Chapter Seven ~ The Review

Test Completion ~ Your Philosophy and Principles

_____
_____
_____
_____
_____
_____
_____
_____
_____
_____
_____
_____
_____
_____
_____
_____
_____
_____
_____
_____
_____
_____
_____
_____
_____
_____

Chapter Seven ~ The Review

~~~~~~~~~~~~~~~~

Test Completion ~ Your Measurable Acton Plan (MAP)

~~~~~~~~~~~~~~~~~~~~~~~~~~~~~~~~~

_____

_____

_____

_____

_____

_____

_____

_____

_____

_____

_____

_____

_____

_____

_____

_____

_____

_____

_____

_____

_____

_____

_____

_____

Chapter Seven ~ The Review

Test Completion ~ Your Measurable Acton Plan (MAP)

Chapter Seven ~ The Review

~~~~~~~~~~~~~~~~

Test Completion ~ Your Measurable Acton Plan (MAP)

~~~~~~~~~~~~~~~~~~~~~~~~~~~~

_____

_____

_____

_____

_____

_____

_____

_____

_____

_____

_____

_____

_____

_____

_____

_____

_____

_____

_____

_____

_____

_____

_____

_____

_____

_____

_____

_____

Chapter Seven ~ The Review

Test Completion ~ Your Measurable Acton Plan (MAP)

Chapter Seven ~ The Review

~~~~~~~~~~~~~~~~~~

Test Completion ~ Your Measurable Acton Plan (MAP)

~~~~~~~~~~~~~~~~~~~~~~~~~~~~~~

_____

_____

_____

_____

_____

_____

_____

_____

_____

_____

_____

_____

_____

_____

_____

_____

_____

_____

_____

_____

_____

_____

_____

Chapter Seven ~ The Review

~~~~~~~~~~~~~~~~~

Test Completion ~ Your Measurable Acton Plan (MAP)

~~~~~~~~~~~~~~~~~~~~~~~~~~~~~~~

_____

_____

_____

_____

_____

_____

_____

_____

_____

_____

_____

_____

_____

_____

_____

_____

_____

_____

_____

_____

_____

_____

_____

Chapter Seven ~ The Review

Test Completion ~ Your Measurable Acton Plan (MAP)

_____
_____
_____
_____
_____
_____
_____
_____
_____
_____
_____
_____
_____
_____
_____
_____
_____
_____
_____
_____
_____
_____
_____
_____
_____
_____
_____
_____

Chapter Seven ~ The Review

Test Completion ~ Your Measurable Acton Plan (MAP)

Chapter Seven ~ The Review

~~~~~~~~~~~~~~~~~~

Test Completion ~ Your Most Limiting
Self-Induced Obstacles

~~~~~~~~~~~~~~~~~~~~~~~~~~~~~~~~~

Chapter Seven ~ The Review

Test Completion ~ Your Most Limiting
Self-Induced Obstacles

Chapter Seven ~ The Review

**Test Completion ~ The Beliefs That Will Have
The Greatest Impact On Your Self and Life**

_____

_____

_____

_____

_____

_____

_____

_____

_____

_____

_____

_____

_____

_____

_____

_____

_____

_____

_____

_____

_____

_____

_____

Chapter Seven ~ The Review

Test Completion ~ The Environments That Will Have The Greatest Impact On Your Self and Life

Chapter Seven ~ The Review

Test Completion ~ The Actions That Will Have The Greatest Impact On Your Self and Life

_____

_____

_____

_____

_____

_____

_____

_____

_____

_____

_____

_____

_____

_____

_____

_____

_____

_____

_____

_____

_____

_____

_____

_____

Chapter Seven ~ The Review

Test Completion ~ The Conditioned Responses That Will Have The Greatest Impact On Your Self and Life

Chapter Seven ~ The Review

~~~~~~~~~~~~~~~~

Test Completion ~ The Habits That Will Have The Greatest Impact On Your Self and Life

~~~~~~~~~~~~~~~~~~~~~~~~~~~~~~~~

_____

_____

_____

_____

_____

_____

_____

_____

_____

_____

_____

_____

_____

_____

_____

_____

_____

_____

_____

_____

_____

_____

_____

Journaling Notes

Journaling Notes

Journaling Notes

Journaling Notes

Journaling Notes

Journaling Notes

Journaling Notes

Journaling Notes

Journaling Notes

Journaling Notes

Journaling Notes

Made in the USA
Monee, IL
11 February 2025

12064617R00089